The Mexican War

A Proud Heritage The Hispanic Library

The Mexican War

How the United States Gained Its Western Lands

Carrie Nichols Cantor

Published in the United States of America by The Child's World®
PO Box 326 • Chanhassen, MN 55317-0326 • 800-599-READ • www.childsworld.com

Acknowledgments
    The Creative Spark: Mary Francis-DeMarois, Project Director; Carrie Nichols Cantor, Series
    Editor; Robert Court, Design and Art Direction
    Carmen Blanco, Curriculum Adviser
    The Child's World®: Mary Berendes, Publishing Director

Photos
    AFP/CORBIS: 34; Craig Aurness/CORBIS: 12; William A. Bake/CORBIS: 16; Bancroft Library-
    University of California, Berkeley: 9, 32, 33; Carrie Nichols Cantor: 7, 15, 30; CORBIS, pp. 11,
    12, 16, 27, 34; Sandy Felsenthal/CORBIS: 11; Philip Greenspun: 22; Dave G. Houser/CORBIS:
    27; UT Institute of Texan Cultures: 25, 28; Library of Congress: 17, 18, 19, 23, 31; San Jacinto
    Museum of History: cover

Library of Congress Cataloging-in-Publication Data
    Cantor, Carrie Nichols.
    The Mexican War : how the United States gained its western lands / by Carrie Nichols Cantor.
    p. cm. — (A proud heritage)
    Summary: Introduces the Mexican War, also called the Mexican-American War, its
    causes, course of events, and aftermath.
    Includes bibliographical references (p.) and index.
    Contents: A growing nation—The outbreak of war —How the war was fought—The
    result of the war—Timeline—Glossary.
    ISBN 1-56766-176-9 (alk. paper)
    1. Mexican War, 1846–1848—Juvenile literature. [1. Mexican War, 1846–1848.] I. Title.
    II. Proud heritage (Child's World (Firm))
    E404.C25 2003
    973.6'2—dc21   2002151727

Republic
of
Texas

Nueces River

Rio Grande

9

15

28

34

A Growing Nation

Almost all Americans know about some of the wars their country has fought, such as the Revolutionary War, the Civil War, and the Vietnam War. Not nearly as many Americans know that the United States fought a 16-month-long war against Mexico—and that the United States started it.

Most Americans think they know how we got the land that makes up the 50 states. Pilgrims and others from Europe, especially England, sailed across the Atlantic Ocean. They fought with Native Americans and gradually took over more and more land. As those early pioneers went farther west, they crossed into Mexico. The lands that are now New Mexico, Arizona, Utah, Nevada, and California, as well as parts of Colorado, Wyoming, and Kansas, were all part of Mexico. Mexico was once larger than the United States! But that changed dramatically in 1848 after the Mexican War.

How did this war start? Were all Americans in favor of it? How did Mexico lose so much of its land? What did the war mean for the future of the United States and Mexico?

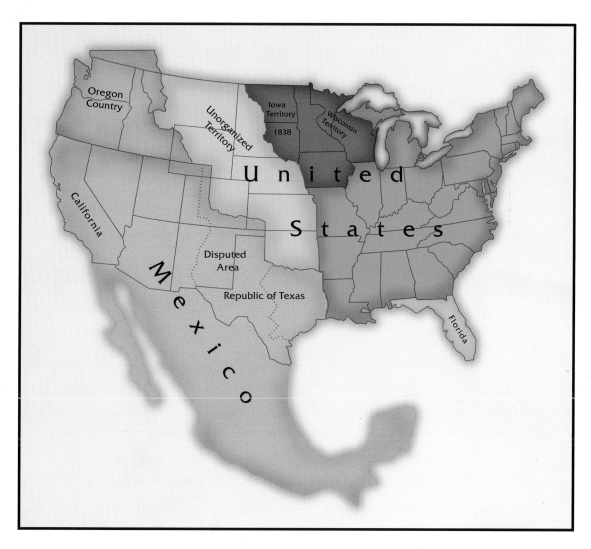

This map shows Mexico's borders in 1840, six years before the beginning of the Mexican War. California, New Mexico, Arizona, and parts of Colorado and Utah were all part of Mexico.

The Pre-War Years

The war officially began in 1846. But to understand it, we must look at what was going on in the years before the first battle.

In the 1800s, the U.S. population was growing rapidly. Many **immigrants** were arriving from other countries. People found a kind of freedom they didn't have elsewhere. In America almost anyone could come and claim land in the West. Of course, they might have to fight Native Americans in order to keep it. America attracted many Europeans who were adventurous and wanted a better life.

Things were different in Mexico. A few people were very rich, and everyone else was very poor. The government gave empty lands to only the Catholic Church and people of pure Spanish blood. There weren't many opportunities for ordinary people, as there were in America.

More and more Americans began settling in the West, on lands that were part of Mexico. Not many Mexicans were settling there. Americans began to feel that the lands should belong to their country, not to Mexico. They were farming, raising cattle, and building towns.

Americans also felt they had a better government than Mexicans. America was a **democracy.** The American people (white men, at least) voted to choose their leaders.

Thousands of Americans made the difficult, dangerous journey from the settled East to the Wild West in the 19th century. Some wanted to stake a claim to land. Others hoped to find gold, get a fresh start, or simply seek adventure.

Mexico was ruled by a series of **dictators** who took control with the help of soldiers. Ordinary Mexican people had no say in what the dictator did or how long he ruled. Most of the Mexican people were poor and powerless.

The Fight over Texas

Much of Mexico's land was far away from the government in Mexico City. The rulers knew they would have a hard time defending these distant lands against Native Americans or other countries. They realized they needed people to settle in Texas. But few Mexicans wanted to live there. The Mexican government began to encourage Americans to settle in Texas starting in 1821.

By 1830, many times more Americans than Mexicans lived in Texas. Most of these Americans did not like being ruled by Mexican dictators. They refused to pay taxes to the Mexican government. Many also kept slaves, despite Mexico's law against slavery. So Mexico's president, General Antonio López de Santa Anna, decided to stop allowing Americans to move to Texas. That made Texans furious.

Then, in 1836, Texans declared Texas was no longer part of Mexico. Santa Anna sent soldiers to Texas. In San Antonio, 189 Texans were killed defending a fort called the Alamo. More than 300 other Texans were killed at a place called Goliad.

Texans and Mexicans fought a number of bloody battles. The Texans went into battle crying, "Remember the Alamo!" to inspire each other. A few months later, the Texan army crushed the Mexican army and captured Santa

Almost 200 Texans died defending the fort called the Alamo, shown in this photograph. The Texans lost that battle but ended up winning the war for Texas a few months later.

The San Jacinto Monument in La Porte, Texas, marks the site of the 1836 battle in which Texas defeated the Mexican Army and won its independence.

Anna in the Battle of San Jacinto. The Mexican ruler had to agree to let Texas go. Texas became a new country called the Republic of Texas (also the Lone Star Republic). Its leaders and most of its people were Americans.

The United States was very different from Mexico. It was growing and getting richer, while Mexico was shrinking and remained poor. The United States had an elected government. Mexico's government kept changing, usually through violence. And Mexicans were frequently at war with each other.

Manifest Destiny

Many Americans wanted to see the United States stretch from the Atlantic Ocean all the way to the Pacific Ocean—from "sea to shining sea." One newspaper writer wrote it was America's "manifest destiny" to keep growing westward all the way to the Pacific Ocean. In other words, it was something that *should* happen and *had* to happen. Americans felt that their country was better and more successful than Mexico, and so they deserved the land. Many Americans had racist and anti-Catholic feelings toward Mexicans as well.

The U.S. government hoped that it could convince Mexico to sell the lands. But many Americans were willing to fight to take them if Mexico would not sell them. Relations between the United States and Mexico grew tense. Mexicans were still angry about Texas. Even after ten years, they still thought of Texas as a part of Mexico.

What brought on the war? It happened when the U.S. government finally invited Texas to become a state.

The Outbreak of War

Mexico still hoped to win back Texas. Troops were positioned at the border, and fights between Mexican soldiers and Texan soldiers sometimes broke out. Making matters worse, Texas was claiming that its southern border with Mexico was along the Rio Grande. Mexico did not agree. In fact, most people, in both the United States and Mexico, had generally agreed that the border was farther north, along the Nueces River. By claiming a border at the Rio Grande, Texas made itself twice as big.

Worst of all for Mexico was the possibility that Texas would join the United States. Gaining Texas would make it bigger, stronger, and more dangerous than ever.

The Antislavery North

The Mexicans were not the only ones who were opposed to Texas's becoming a state. Northerners in the United

States did not want another Southern state in the Union. The North and the South had different opinions about many things. Their biggest disagreement was over slavery. The North did not want another slave state. That would make the South more powerful and expand slavery.

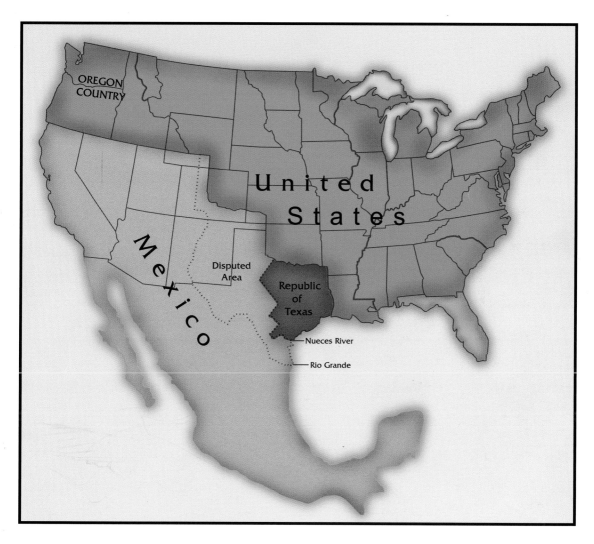

Mexico claimed Texas only went as far south as the Nueces River. The Republic of Texas (1836–1845) claimed the border was at the Rio Grande.

For ten years, the Lone Star Republic (Texas) tried to become a state. But the North kept this from happening. Finally, though, Southern politicians got their way. Just before he left office, President John Tyler and the U.S. Congress offered statehood to Texas. The new president, James K. Polk, was in favor of it. (Both presidents were

The Rio Grande is the present border between Texas and Mexico.

from the South.) Texans voted on July 4, 1845, to enter the Union as the 28th state.

The new U.S. president in 1845, James K. Polk, favored allowing Texas to become a state.

The United States then got ready to **annex** Texas, or make Texas officially part of the United States. President Polk sent soldiers, led by General Zachary Taylor, down to the Texas-Mexico border in case of war with Mexico.

At the same time, President Polk felt strongly that the United States had to expand to the west. He wanted to buy the lands of New Mexico and California from Mexico. Polk offered to pay millions of dollars for them. But the Mexican government would not even discuss the offer.

Attempts at Peace

The man who was then Mexico's president, General José Joaquín Herrera, was not eager for war. Although Mexico had a much larger army than the United States and its soldiers were very experienced, wars cost money.

President Herrera hoped to come to an agreement in order to avoid war.

But Herrera was pushed out of power by another general named Mariano Paredes y Arrillaga. General Paredes and his supporters wanted to go to war with the United States.

Congressman Abraham Lincoln, who would years later become president of the United States, spoke out against the idea of war with Mexico.

Meanwhile, not all Americans wanted war with Mexico. Many people felt it was wrong to fight their neighbor to take its land. Some felt a democracy should not be fighting at all—that the United States was a land of liberty and justice, not of war and conquest. John Quincy Adams, a former president, tried to get Congress to cut off the money for the war. Congressman Abraham Lincoln called the war "unconstitutional," or against U.S. law.

Zachary Taylor was born on November 24, 1784, and grew up on a Kentucky plantation. His father, a slave owner, was active in state politics. Taylor had little schooling but great intelligence. He became famous fighting in the Seminole War (1835–1842) against Native Americans in Florida.

Taylor was a brave man who never sent his soldiers where he himself would not go. He was 62 years old when he went down to Mexico to lead a force of 3,500 men. His speech was rough and full of mistakes. A short and heavy man, he had little concern for proper dress. In fact, he was sloppy. He wore a faded uniform and a big, old straw hat. His men affectionately called him "Old Rough and Ready."

During the first year of the Mexican War, Taylor won several important battles in northern Mexico. He was cele-brated as a war hero back home. When the war was over, he ran for president and won. He became the 12th president in 1849, but served for only 18 months. He died of a stom-ach ailment (possibly cholera) on July 9, 1850.

Moving toward War

Because of the antiwar feelings, President Polk could not just send soldiers storming into Mexico. He had to wait for the right moment. He knew that he could not get the whole country to support the war unless Mexico started it.

So he ordered General Zachary Taylor to move his soldiers into the area south of the Nueces River that Texas had been claiming. Mexicans considered this land part of Mexico. No one was surprised when Mexico attacked and killed some U.S. soldiers in this disputed area. Now President Polk could argue that Mexicans had killed Americans on "American soil." This way, it sounded as if America had been attacked by Mexico, and so America had to defend itself. Though not exactly true, it worked.

The U.S. Congress told the president to go ahead and fight Mexico. Polk signed the declaration of war on May 13, 1846.

Chapter Three

How the War Was Fought

The Mexican War was fought entirely on Mexican soil. Ordinary Mexicans suffered greatly. General Taylor's army quickly won its first few battles and moved deeper into Mexico. From May 1846 through the end of the year, Taylor battled his way through northern Mexico. The Mexicans put up some brave fights but did not win any battles. The Americans kept moving forward. By the end of the autumn, Taylor's forces had captured the capitals of three northern Mexican states.

The Fall of California and New Mexico

With the Mexican army busy fighting General Taylor, there were no government troops to protect Mexico's faraway lands. That summer, both California and New Mexico were taken by American forces. Some *Californios* (Mexicans living in California) fought back. They wanted California to be an independent country, not a part of the United States. They were not strong enough to win, but they forced the United States to battle for California. New Mexico, on the other hand, surrendered without a fight. The governor, who was supposed to find men to fight to defend New Mexico, simply ran away.

With the war not going well, General Paredes was thrown out of power in Mexico. The same General Santa Anna who had ordered the Texans killed at the Alamo became president once again.

The Spanish had a strong presence in California. This beautiful mission, or church, was founded in Santa Barbara in 1782.

The March to Mexico City

In January 1847, a new phase of the war began. President Polk realized that Mexico would not give up unless the United States took Mexico City itself. Taylor's forces in northern Mexico were too far from the capital city. So President Polk sent ships carrying new troops to the port of Veracruz, in central Mexico. He sent his general-in-chief, General Winfield Scott, down to Mexico to take half of General Taylor's men and meet up with the new force. Scott and his men promptly conquered the walled city of Veracruz and then continued advancing toward the capital.

The war lasted for about nine more months. Americans hoped that, as their army got closer and closer to Mexico City, the Mexicans would surrender. But Santa Anna would not give in. The bloody battles continued.

In September 1847, the war finally reached a critical point. General Scott's forces

General Winfield Scott led the U.S. troops into the heart of Mexico.

Surely one of the most deceitful, **brutal,** and colorful characters in Mexican history was General Antonio López de Santa Anna (1794–1876). A military hero, he became president of Mexico for the first time in 1832. He promptly threw out Mexico's constitution.

He brutally crushed the Texas rebellion in 1836 to teach the Texans a lesson. Captured by the Texans during the Battle of San Jacinto, he was nearly executed. But the leader of the Texas army agreed to spare him. Santa Anna then convinced Texas's president that if he was allowed to return to Mexico City, he would speak out in favor of Texas's independence. He didn't keep this promise.

When he returned to Mexico, he found there was a new president. Another general had seized power.

Two years later, Santa Anna was hit by a cannonball fired from a French ship and lost his lower left leg. He made up a story about the battle, portraying himself as a hero, and was carried off to Mexico City to become president once again. In 1842, he had his leg dug up and given a fancy state funeral!

By 1844, people turned against him again and threw him out in favor of General Herrera, the man who tried to prevent war with the United States. Santa Anna went into **exile** in Cuba.

In the summer of 1846, Santa Anna was in secret contact with U.S. president Polk. He promised Polk that if the United States allowed him to return to Mexico, he would seize power, end the war, and sell the United States the lands it wanted.

Meanwhile, many Mexicans became unhappy with the new president, General Paredes, who had overthrown Herrera. Santa Anna was able to take over the government once again. Contrary to his promise, he vowed to fight against America to keep Mexico's lands.

After he was defeated by the Americans in Mexico City in September 1847, Santa Anna went into exile again, in what must have seemed like his final exit. But he became president of Mexico again in 1853! He then sold more territory to the United States simply because he needed money. He was later sent into exile again but was allowed to come home before he died in 1876.

were now right outside Mexico City. American and Mexican officials had been talking since April, trying to end the war. But the talks had failed. The Americans knew they would have to capture Mexico City to force the Mexicans to surrender. The soldiers were exhausted. There were fewer and fewer of them alive and healthy enough to keep fighting. Yet they would now have to fight a Mexican army that was protecting the very heart of its country—its oldest and largest city.

Santa Anna, meanwhile, had even worse problems. The enemy was at the gates, and a rival Mexican general was threatening his life!

Then there was a temporary peace. General Scott and Santa Anna agreed to an **armistice** so that the two sides could try to settle their differences. The talks did not succeed. The one thing the Mexicans would not agree to was the Rio Grande border for Texas. Even though Santa Anna knew Mexico would lose the war, he was afraid that if he gave in to the Americans, he would be accused of **treason** by his generals. So the war went on.

Despite heroic efforts by some Mexicans, an important castle right outside Mexico City, the Castle of Chapultepec, fell to the Americans. Just a few hours later, U.S. troops entered Mexico City.

On the western edge of Mexico City, on top of a hill, is an enormous castle, the Castle of Chapultepec. In 1847, it housed a military school. General Scott decided to attack the castle before entering the city. First, 500 soldiers carried ladders to the base of the castle and climbed up its walls. The rest of the fighting force then followed them up. Americans fought Mexicans face-to-face inside the castle in a bloody battle.

When it became clear the Americans were winning, many Mexican soldiers ran away. Some of the teenaged cadets (soldiers in training) stayed to fight. According to legend, six chose to die rather than surrender. One of them wrapped himself in the Mexican flag and jumped to his death from the castle wall. The six are called the *Niños Heroes* (boy heroes) and are honored every year in Mexico with a ceremony. Mexicans are reminded of them whenever they pass the monument in Chapultepec Park (pictured above). The six columns honor each of the six boys.

The U.S. troops were close to total victory when they took the Castle of Chapultepec right outside Mexico City.

That night, on September 13, 1847, Santa Anna resigned as president. Early the next morning, a group of Mexican leaders went to General Scott's headquarters to surrender their capital city. Finally the fighting was over.

Now it was time to **negotiate** a treaty. It took months for both sides to agree. The Treaty of Guadalupe Hidalgo was signed on February 2, 1848. By the end of July, all U.S. troops had left Mexico.

Chapter Four

Results of the War

The war devastated Mexico. It lost Upper California and New Mexico and was forced to agree to the Rio Grande border for Texas. In return, it was paid $15 million so that the United States could say it bought the land and did not take it by force. The United States allowed Mexico to keep Lower California (Baja California) and a small area of land connecting it to Mexico. Some Americans called for the United States to annex all of Mexico! Others felt it wasn't right to take any land at all.

In a letter, Lieutenant Ulysses S. Grant wrote about American volunteer soldiers who had arrived in camp and seemed to "enjoy acts of violence." He said they had murdered a startling number of ordinary Mexicans. These brutal acts against innocent people were not reported in the newspapers back home. Most people did not see this ugly side of the war.

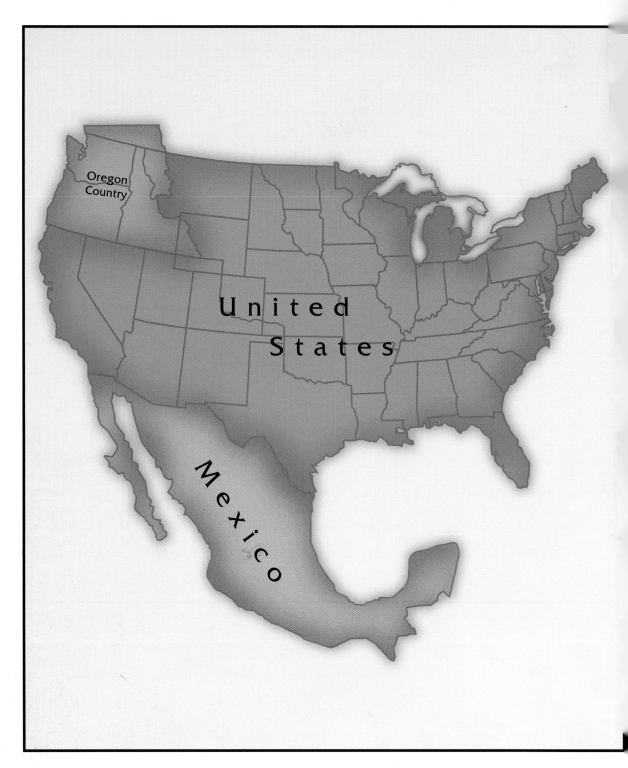

The United States became much bigger and Mexico much smaller after the two countries signed the Treaty of Guadalupe Hidalgo in 1848.

The Two Sides

One can argue that Mexico didn't have a much greater right to the lands than the United States. In fact, all of the land in the Americas had been taken by force from the Native Americans. The Spanish had killed and displaced millions of Native Americans in order to create New Spain.

After winning its independence from Spain in 1821, Mexico wasn't strong enough to take care of its vast territory. Americans had built thriving communities in many Mexican lands. Was it right that these Americans were ruled by a Mexican dictator? Was it right that they

Ulysses S. Grant on the Mexican War

Lieutenant Ulysses S. Grant (1822–1885) thought about resigning from the army to protest the war with Mexico, but he didn't. Grant was not the only officer who opposed the war. But he did his job anyway and did it extremely well, serving under General Taylor. He eventually became a general and led the North to victory in the Civil War years later. In 1869, he became president of the United States, serving two terms.

Railroads united the eastern and western areas of the United States.

had to pay taxes to a far-off government that didn't build roads or protect them? There was right and wrong on both sides.

In the decades that followed the war, the United States finished building railroads across the continent. People and products were then able to move around the country more easily. Trade exploded. With all the buying and selling across thousands of miles, the country got richer and more powerful. Trade with other countries also increased. The Pacific ports in California made it easier for America to trade with Asia.

More than 13,000 Americans died in the war, and thousands more were horribly wounded. But the United States gained a territory five times the size of France. The Mexicans lost many more men and had nothing to show for it. Americans quickly forgot about the war with Mexico.

The Gold Rush

When gold was discovered in California in 1848, millions of people rushed to seek their fortune there. They were called "Forty-Niners" because so many of them arrived in the year 1849. California had been part of Mexico until the war. If Mexico had not lost its lands in the war, it would have owned all that gold and gained all those new settlers.

U.S. president George W. Bush (right) sits with Mexican president Vicente Fox. Today Mexico and the United States are close allies.

The arguments in the United States between North and South continued to heat up, and the Civil War finally broke out in 1861.

Mexico did not quickly forget. The war left its people bitter and resentful for decades. Fortunately, peace has reigned on the border for more than 150 years, and the two countries now have a friendly relationship.

- "From the halls of Montezuma to the shores of Tripoli . . ." is the first line from "The Marines' Hymn." The halls of Montezuma refers to the Castle of Chapultepec outside Mexico City, which was occupied by U.S. forces in 1847. Montezuma was the Aztec leader who was conquered by the Spanish in the 16th century.

- Approximately 75,000 Mexicans were living in the lands that the United States took over after the war.

- Among Mexico's best fighters was a group of about 700 Irishmen known as the *San Patricios* (Spanish for St. Patricks). They had recently immigrated to the United States and had immediately volunteered to join the U.S. army. Stationed at the U.S.-Mexico border under General Taylor, they were treated very badly by soldiers who did not respect them because they were both foreign and Catholic. These Irishmen turned against the United States and fought bravely for the Mexicans.

- Most of the more than 13,000 Americans who lost their lives in the war died of disease or as a result of an accident. Only one in eight was killed by the Mexicans.

- During the entire war and the treaty talks, the United States had one leader, President Polk. During the same period, Mexico had seven. Mexico's generals fought more battles against each other than against the Americans.

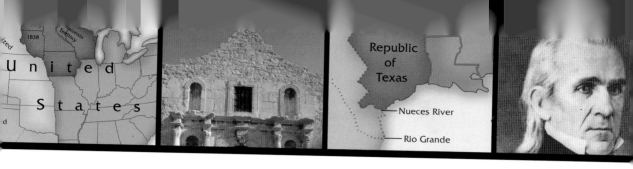

1492: Christopher Columbus, sailing for Spain, discovers the Americas.

1519–21: The Spanish conquer the Aztecs in the area today known as Mexico. The city of Mexico (now called Mexico City) is built on the ruins of the Aztec capital city.

1607: British settlers set up the first British colony in the Americas, at Jamestown, Virginia.

1776: The 13 American colonies take up arms against the British to win their independence.

1803: The United States doubles the size of its territory with the Louisiana Purchase, buying a vast western area from France for $15 million.

1810: Mexicans begin an 11-year fight to gain their independence from Spain.

1821: Mexico becomes an independent nation. Its government begins encouraging Americans to settle in the Mexican state of Texas.

1836: In March, Texas declares its independence from Mexico. Texans are killed at the Alamo and at Goliad.

In April, Texas defeats Mexico at the Battle of San Jacinto. Texas becomes the Lone Star Republic, an independent country.

1845: In March, the U.S. government offers Texas statehood, just days before a new president, James K. Polk, takes office. General Zachary Taylor and U.S. troops are sent down to the border in case of war.

In July, Texas votes to become the 28th state to enter the Union.

1846: In April, fighting breaks out in the disputed area between Texas and Mexico, north of the Rio Grande.

In May, the United States declares war on Mexico.

In August, U.S. armed forces take New Mexico and enter California. Throughout the summer and fall, General Taylor keeps advancing south.

In September, Mexico's general Santa Anna seizes power in Mexico City.

1847: In January, the Treaty of Cahuenga ends the California conflict.

In March, U.S. general Winfield Scott is sent to central Mexico, takes Veracruz, and begins advancing toward Mexico City.

In September, General Scott's forces occupy Mexico City.

1848: In February, the United States and Mexico sign the Treaty of Guadalupe Hidalgo. Mexico loses New Mexico and Upper California and has to accept the Rio Grande border for Texas, in exchange for $15 million.

1854: The United States buys 30,000 square miles (77,700 square kilometers) of Mexican land south of Arizona and New Mexico through an agreement known as the Gadsden Purchase.

annex (an-NEKS) To annex an area of land, a country begins to treat that land and its people as part of it. Mexico's leaders were upset when the United States began to annex Texas, because they knew it would be difficult to get Texas back.

armistice (AR-miss-tiss) An armistice is an agreement between two warring countries to stop fighting while they work out a treaty. The United States and Mexico agreed to an armistice in September 1847, but fighting broke out again later.

brutal (BROO-tuhl) A brutal act is cruel and violent. Some Americans committed brutal acts against Mexicans.

democracy (deh-MOK-ruh-see) A country is a democracy if its people vote to elect their leaders. Countries that don't have democracy are typically ruled by a king, queen, or dictator who remains in power for life.

dictators (DIK-tay-turz) Dictators are people who rule over a country through force. For a long time, Mexico was ruled by dictators.

exile (EKS-zyl) When someone goes into exile, he flees his country and has to live somewhere else. General Santa Anna kept doing things that made Mexican people angry, and so he had to go into exile several times.

immigrants (IH-meh-grents) Immigrants are people who have moved to a country from some other country. About half of General Taylor's soldiers were immigrants to the United States, many from Ireland.

negotiate (nuh-GOH-shee-ayt) To negotiate is to talk about differences and try to reach a solution. Mexicans and Americans did negotiate during the war, but they could not agree on a solution to their conflict.

treason (TREE-zun) Treason is the crime of betraying one's nation. In many countries, the punishment for treason is death.

Books

Carter, Alden, R. *The Mexican War.* New York: Franklin Watts, 1992.

Collier, Christopher, and James Lincoln Collier. *Hispanic America, Texas, and the Mexican War: 1835–1850.* Tarrytown, N.Y.: Benchmark Book, 1999.

Jacobs, William Jay. *War with Mexico.* Brookfield, Conn.: Millbrook Press, 1993.

Nardo, Don. *The Mexican-American War.* Farmington Hills, Mich.: Lucent Books, 1999.

Web Sites

Visit our Web page for lots of links about the Mexican War:
http://www.childsworld.com/links.html

Note to parents, teachers, and librarians: We routinely monitor our Web links to make sure they're safe, active sites.

Sources Used by the Author

Christensen, Carol, and Thomas Christensen. *The U.S.-Mexican War* (Companion to the Public Television Series *The U.S.-Mexican War, 1846–1848).* San Francisco: Bay Books, 1998.

Fernandez-Shaw, Carlos. *The Hispanic Presence in North America from 1492 to Today.* Trans. by Alfonso Bertodano Stourton and others. New York: Facts on File, 1987.

Leckie, Robert. *From Sea to Shining Sea: From the War of 1812 to the Mexican War, the Saga of America's Expansion.* New York: HarperCollins Publishers, 1993.

Novas, Himilce. *Everything You Need to Know about Latino History.* New York: Plume, 1994.

Werstein, Irving. *The War with Mexico.* New York: W. W. Norton & Company, 1965.

Zinn, Howard. *A People's History of the United States: 1492–Present.* Twentieth Anniversary Edition. New York: HarperCollins, 1999.

Index